FRANKLIN PARK PUBLIC LIBRARY

3 1316 00423 637

W9-AYA-508

12/13

REPORTER IN DISGUISE:
The Intrepid Vic Steinberg

CHRISTINE WELLDON

FRANKLIN PARK LIBRARY
WITHDRAWN

Fitzhenry & Whiteside

To storytellers and listeners everywhere.

"Three apples fell from the sky...
one for the teller, one for the listener
and one for the child who might
some day read it in a book."

~ Turkish expression ~

A special thanks to

Peggy Perdue, Special Collections, Toronto Reference Library;
Harriet Xanthakos, storyteller extraordinaire;
and peerless editors Solange Messier and Christie Harkin.

Text copyright © 2013 Christine Welldon

Published in Canada by Fitzhenry & Whiteside,
195 Allstate Parkway, Markham, Ontario L3R 4T8

Published in the United States by Fitzhenry & Whiteside,
311 Washington Street, Brighton, Massachusetts 02135

All rights reserved. No part of this book may be reproduced in any manner without the express
written consent of the publisher, except in the case of brief excerpts in critical reviews and articles.
All inquiries should be addressed to Fitzhenry & Whiteside Limited, 195 Allstate Parkway, Markham, Ontario L3R 4T8.
www.fitzhenry.ca   godwit@fitzhenry.ca

J-B
STEINBERG
423-6371

10 9 8 7 6 5 4 3 2 1

Library and Archives Canada Cataloguing in Publication
Welldon, Christine
Reporter in disguise : the intrepid Vic Steinberg
/ Christine Welldon.
Includes bibliographical references and index.
ISBN 978-1-55455-233-7 (bound).--ISBN 978-1-55455-281-8 (pbk.)
1. Steinberg, Vic--Juvenile literature. 2. Journalists--Canada--
Biography--Juvenile literature. 3. Women journalists--Canada--
Biography--Juvenile literature. I. Title.
PN4913.S74W44 2012   j070.92   C2012-906822-5

Publisher Cataloging-in-Publication Data (U.S.)
Welldon, Christine.
Reporter in disguise: the intrepid Vic Steinberg / Christine Welldon.
[88] p. : ill., photos. ; cm.
Includes bibliographical references and index.
Summary: A look into the life of a secretive and feisty woman who broke ground
by pursuing a career in investigative journalism.
ISBN: 978-1-55455-233-7
ISBN: 978-1-55455-281-8 (pbk.)
1. Steinberg, Vic – Juvenile literature.
2. Journalists – Canada – Biography – Juvenile literature.
3. Women journalists – Canada – Biography – Juvenile literature. I. Title.
070.92 [B] dc23   PN4874.S74W45 2012

Fitzhenry & Whiteside acknowledges with thanks the Canada Council for the Arts,
and the Ontario Arts Council for their support of our publishing program. We acknowledge the financial support
of the Government of Canada through the Canada Book Fund (CBF) for our publishing activities.

Cover and interior design by Tanya Montini
Cover images courtesy of: Queen's Hotel: McLeod & Simpson; Silhouette: Shutterstock; Newspaper: John Robarts Library
Printed by Sheck Wah Tong Printing Press Ltd. in China in January 2013
Job #65461

Table of Contents

Credit: Library and Archives Canada

Can you guess why Toronto was called The Big Smoke?

"It is not ladylike, you say, to go to report a police court case?
It is not proper to walk the streets at midnight, and so forth?
Well and good. If so, no women need apply to work on even terms
with men. They may do odds and ends of work and be paid accordingly.
But if a girl means to be a journalist, she ought to be
a journalist out and out, and not try to be
a journalist up to nine o' clock."[1]

—W.T. Stead

Foreword

I first met Vic Steinberg at Mackenzie House, once the home of publisher and Toronto's very first mayor, William Lyon Mackenzie. "Vic" came into the room dressed as a maid and she entertained us with the story of how she, a top reporter, had disguised herself in this way to work in a Toronto home. She was badly mistreated there, and she told us about it. She went on to describe similar adventures—pretending to be a seamstress in a sweatshop, where she earned only one and two-thirds cents for the whole day's work; and even dressing as a man to enter a tavern! Story after story followed, and I listened intently, captivated by her daring and sense of mischief. Of course, it wasn't really Vic I was listening to! Vic lived in the 19th century, after all. The individual who had captured my imagination was a talented storyteller named Harriet Xanthakos. She had studied Vic's writings and was now telling Vic's stories. I asked Harriet where she had found these stories and she told me they were from Vic's newspaper columns housed at the John Robarts Library in Toronto. Harriet kindly sent me copies and I read them with eager interest. There are many details we do not know about this secretive and feisty journalist—we don't even know her real name!—but one thing we know for sure, Vic Steinberg would be laughing if she knew that decades after her death, people are still wondering about her and trying to solve the puzzle that was her life.

While Vic always kept her private life and identity a secret, in her columns I found revealing clues about her, clues that Vic probably didn't even notice she had left. This book is the result of all my reading and research about Vic Steinberg and Victorian Toronto. Each chapter begins with a story, which I created from these clues. What other clues to her identity can you find?

Who was Vic Steinberg?

It was a grey, wintry morning in Toronto. The crowded streetcar made its way along College Street, filled with early morning

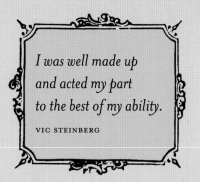

> *I was well made up and acted my part to the best of my ability.*
>
> VIC STEINBERG

passengers on their way to work. "I've heard Vic Steinberg is actually a society lady," a woman was saying, glancing over at her husband's newspaper to note that he was reading the *Vic Steinberg* column. A passenger standing nearby looked sharply over at the two and moved in closer to listen. "They say she is a tall woman, a spinster, grey-haired, about fifty or so, and very plain. That makes it easy to disguise herself as a man, I would imagine."

"I'll tell you my idea," said her husband. "My idea is that this Vic Steinberg is…a man."

"Perhaps she is," agreed his wife. "She is almost too…too venturesome for a woman—and these articles are not quite in a woman's style; they are too…too full of dash, you know."

"Yes," replied her husband. "More like the writings of the American journalists. In fact, I imagine Vic Steinberg is an American."

Just then, the conductor called out, "Sherbourne Street!"

The eavesdropper began to smile and a twinkle of mischief lit up her expression. She peered out the window and noticed she was at her stop. She had to reach up to ring the bell, brushing aside a stray tendril of her unruly brown hair as she did so. She pulled up the hood of her cape to cover her head, then

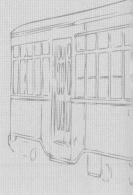

Credit: City of Toronto Archives, Fonds 16, Series 71, Item 3368

Streetcars were horse-drawn until 1893 when the first electric streetcar was invented. It took several years to phase out horse-drawn streetcars in Toronto.

quickly dropped a business card into the woman's lap, just as the streetcar rumbled to a stop. The card read "Vic Steinberg, Reporter, *Toronto News.*"

The passenger pushed through the crowd, stifling a giggle as she heard an exclamation of surprise from the young wife, who turned her head to try and catch a glimpse of her—but was not quick enough.

What story is she pursuing this time? wondered the woman. Who is she really? Everyone knew that Vic Steinberg was a master of disguise....But it was too late. The passenger was long gone.

───────

Who was Vic Steinberg—fortune teller? Shop girl? Seamstress? Vic Steinberg wore many disguises but no one except her close friends and colleagues knew her real name. Vic was a rare phenomenon: the woman newspaper columnist. And more than that, she was the only reporter at her paper to have her own byline. In the Victorian Age, a time when women were destined for marriage and homemaking, women columnists were almost unheard of. Vic worked for the *Toronto News*, a paper that middle- and working-class people read because they had a liking for sensational stories, local gossip, and crime. When the paper hit the front porches, readers would turn to her column before reading the news of the day. In 1890s Toronto, who else could take women to places they had never been—the sweatshops, the men's smoking rooms, the taverns? Vic Steinberg entered these places without fear, then reported back with a special blend of humour and curiosity that made her readers want to know more.

Vic didn't care about the dresses women were wearing that season, or who was holding a garden party this summer. She had no interest in women's hats or the latest kitchen gadgets. Instead, she was determined to go to places where women of "class" did not go. She could only do these daring things if she kept her identity a secret. Disguising herself gave her the freedom to blend in with people from all walks of life. Sometimes she explored Toronto dressed as a man, but she always wrote from a woman's point of view.

She would frown if anyone called her a "stunt" reporter. She gave herself a much more respectable title; Vic Steinberg, investigative reporter.

Vic Steinberg probably started out on the beat, covering criminal cases and spending time in the police courts. When she became a columnist, she had fun reporting on how men behave when they are away from their wives in the taverns and at sports events. She soon began to report on the unfairness she found in everyday life—the hard lives of domestic servants, the miserable experience of seamstresses, the conditions in the women's prison.

It didn't take long for Vic's readership to grow.

ic Steinberg's paper, the *Toronto News* was a sister paper of the *Toronto Mail*. While the *Mail* was read by the upper classes, *The News* was written for the middle and lower working classes. It covered sensational stories, local gossip, and crime. Reporters from *The News* spent much of their time in police courts, reporting on criminal cases, because their readers enjoyed gossiping about local crimes.

Credit: Wikimedia Commons

"Read all about it!" Toronto readers liked to find out the latest in sensational stories, local gossip, and crime.

None of her readers ever discovered Vic Steinberg's real name or true identity, though there were many guesses. Vic knew that as long as people were wondering about her, it meant that people were reading her column.

So, how did she do it? How did she remain such a mystery and capture the curiosity and interest of everyone who read her? And did she know there were clues about her, scattered among her columns? If you read carefully "between the lines," you can find out some information about this feisty reporter.

There were three classes of people in Victorian times. The upper class was wealthy and usually lived on inherited money. The middle classes worked in business and lived well as long as they kept working. The lower classes were not educated and usually worked in jobs that did not require special skills. They earned little and lived very simply.

The invention of the linotype in 1886 meant that newspapers were being printed into the thousands instead of the hundreds. Now, households in every part of Ontario were receiving daily newspapers and there were women in those households who were interested in buying the newest kitchen gadget, or learning about the latest fashions.

Ottmar Mergenthaler invented the linotype composing machine, a printing machine that could set type and print newspapers by the thousands. It was first used by the *New York Tribune* in 1886.

Chapter 1

Vic at the Rugby Game

As Vic entered the men's smoking car, she began to breathe in clouds of tobacco smoke. Her heart pounded as boisterous laughter and loud voices spilled around her, and she felt a chill of fear because she was the only woman in a smoking car full of men. She caught sight of her reflection in the mirrored glass and saw that her disguise was so perfect that she had a hard time recognizing herself amongst the men. She felt suddenly much calmer. Today, she was one of "them,"—one of the boys.

Her friend Ned had lent her a casual suit and tie, checkered trousers, vest and jacket, and blue cravat. Her trousers were too long and she had changed the buttons and hitched them higher by shortening her braces under the vest and jacket. She had pinned up her hair tightly under the brown derby so that not a stray lock could be seen, and she carried a walking stick bearing the colourful ribbons of the Queen's team she was supporting: red, blue, and yellow.

Vic was on her way to a rugby match in Hamilton. Without her disguise, she would at this very moment have been

> *I have always fancied that the boys enjoyed a game better than we women and, I confess it, I had strongly desired to enjoy the pleasures of seeing a big Rugby battle untrammeled by the restrictions applying to our sex.*
>
> *I wanted to see the game with the eyes of a man—or at least from his standpoint.*
>
> *I was puffing another of those horrid cigarettes, for it seemed my fate to have them constantly proffered.*
>
> VIC STEINBERG

Credit: Frederic Humbert

These Toronto rugby players are ready to win.

sitting in the non-smoking car, quietly gazing out of the train window, and feeling the tightness of her corset under her long day dress. Instead, here she was, corset free, and standing shoulder to shoulder with men who puffed on cigarettes and cigars and argued about the strengths of the Hamilton Tigers; men who hardly noticed her at all.

She walked boldly down the aisle and threw herself into a seat, keeping her knees slightly apart just the way a man would sit. Ned nudged her and took out his silver case, offering a cigarette. Vic scowled and took one, lit it, and puffed on it, exhaling clouds of smoke. She found the taste disgusting but whenever someone glanced toward her, she took another puff.

So far, things were going well. Raucous laughter rang out from the other end of the car, and she heard good-natured arguments about the Queen's Collegians versus the Hamilton

Credit: Detroit Publishing Co.

Plush seats and comfortable surroundings were typical of the smoking car. Strictly for men, it was a comfortable place to spend time on long train journeys.

Tigers, but no one swore or cursed and there was not a word said that a lady shouldn't hear.

The men around her called the opposing team's players "rotten" or "ragged," and described the coaches as "damn foolish," or "dirty," but their language was no worse than that. Ned had already given her a quick lesson on the game of rugby, and as they travelled along, she went through the rules in her head and tried to list all the terms. Scrim? Or was it scrum? Grubber, offsides, maul…so much to remember!

The train pulled into Hamilton station and Vic piled out with the men. They all climbed into waiting carriages, then bowled along pretty streets to an uptown hotel tavern. There, Vic leaned against the bar with the others.

"How about something to keep the life in you? You know, on the field?" asked a Queen's supporter, offering Vic a glass of ale.

"Not for me," answered Vic, muffling her voice and trying to sound as gruff as she could. "I'm a Temperance man, myself."

She looked around for Ned and he came just in time, placing a glass of juice in front of her. The man looked at her curiously. Had he seen through her disguise? He winked at Ned, as if to say, "What's your racket?"

There was a sudden rush to leave and head for the stadium where two

> **T**he Temperance Union was formed to discourage people from drinking alcohol. It was believed that drinking was sure to break up families and ruin people's lives. The Union encouraged moderation at all times.

thousand people waited for the start of the game. Vic hurried along with the crowd, keeping Ned in sight. Soon she was sitting in the men's area of the stands with other reporters and fans, puffing on another cigarette. Respectable women in the 1890s never smoked, but smoking was an important part of her disguise. She might as well get used to it. The man on one side of her turned to speak to her.

"Are you a Queen's man?" he asked, noticing the colours of her ribbons.

She nodded yes, and gave a grunt of agreement.

"What do you think are their chances? Are they in good shape, do you think?"

Vic blushed and began to stammer. "Well..." She hadn't prepared for this question. Ned hadn't taught her the strengths of each team.

Had she blown her disguise?

But she realized that, of course, she *could* talk about about the Kingston university's athletic spirit, and the healthfulness of the sports program. She would make it all up—she was a writer, wasn't she?

Credit: www.istock.com

This gentleman's outfit shows what Vic might have looked like in her disguise. On her walking stick, she attached the coloured ribbons of the team she supported.

She opened her mouth to begin, but a loud cheer cut her off in mid-sentence as the players entered the field and stood in formation for the kick-off. The man turned his attention away from her to the game. "Saved," she muttered.

But Vic soon forgot that she was pretending to be a man. The game was exciting and she was caught up in the spirit of the crowd. She began to pepper Ned with questions and observations.

"Number six is such a fast runner, they can hardly catch him. Why did they give the Tigers a penalty kick?"

Vic asked one question after another, fascinated by the game, but there came a hissed caution from Ned and a warning grip on her arm. She had been talking like a woman, using her natural voice. She found the game so exciting that she had forgotten she was in disguise.

Two or three men heard her girlish voice amidst the noise and din of the crowd, and were staring hard at her.

Just at that moment, the captain of the Queen's team was tackled until he had to release the ball. Players from both sides rushed for it.

"A perfect touch!" shouted Vic.

"You mean, ruck!" hissed Ned.

Blundered again, thought Vic. She had better just keep quiet for the rest of the game.

The spectators hurled curses, and Vic heard a few "damns" as the Queen's players gradually scored points against the Tigers. At the end of the afternoon, she cheered with everyone else when her team won, but she was not sorry it was over. By this time, Vic was tired of the game and tired of playing at being a man. Her throat was sore from so many cigarettes, her collar band dug into her throat, and her nerves were on edge from all the noise and the stress of constantly acting a part. All she wanted now was to be home in her cozy den, writing up her story.

At last, they boarded the train for Toronto, and Vic sat in a corner and pretended to be asleep.

But she had pulled it off! With more practice it would become so much easier to go about in disguise and visit places no lady would ever see. The only annoyance was those cigarettes! She had to smoke so many if she was to stay in disguise as a man.

The Grey Cup, today a trophy for Canadian professional football supremacy, was originally not a pro award and actually was not intended for football at all! In 1909 all football in Canada was amateur and was governed by the Canadian Rugby Union.

"I puffed courageously," she told her readers. "I went, I saw, I conquered!"

There would be more adventures to come. This was just the start.

⁓⁓⁓

Vic so enjoyed watching the game that she went on to watch many more events, although never again in disguise. The Hamilton Tigers eventually won five Grey Cup championships in succeeding years. When they merged with the Hamilton Wildcats in 1950, the team was renamed the Hamilton Tiger-Cats Football Club. They won the Grey Cup eight more times after the 1950 merger and remain the Tiger-Cats to this day. If Vic were still alive in the 1950s, she probably would have become a big fan of football.

CLUE

This column was Vic's first. Do you think her readers enjoyed it? Why? What are your first impressions of Vic Steinberg as a woman reporter? How would you describe her?

Credit: Library and Archives Canada

The Hamilton Tigers, a Canadian rugby club from 1869 till 1950, battle the Ottawa team in a fierce rugby match.

Chapter 2

Vic Steinberg, Fortune Teller

Madame Vanier

OF CHICAGO,

who has gained celebrity as a

FORTUNE TELLER,

will live at 31 Temperance Street
from Tuesday until Saturday.

Vic hoped this ad would attract some attention. What should she wear? Fortune tellers often looked like Gypsies, so how about hoop earrings, beads and bracelets? Or better still, she could appear as a fashionable woman.

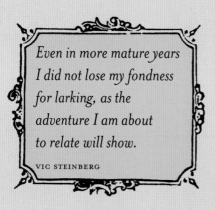

Even in more mature years I did not lose my fondness for larking, as the adventure I am about to relate will show.

VIC STEINBERG

Vic went shopping at Eaton's Department Store and found just the gown for the occasion in apple-green soft wool. It had a high neckline, leg o' mutton sleeves puffed at the shoulders to her elbows, and a skirt that widened and flared to show off the tight waistline. But first, as any good investigative reporter would do, she visited some local fortune tellers to gather a few helpful pointers. She had her own fortune read several times, secretly studying these women as they bent over their cards or gazed at the tea leaves in her cup.

Credit: City of Toronto Archives, Fonds 1244, Item 3059

Vic shopped for her fortune teller disguise at Eaton's. This cozy winter scene depicts the original Eaton's store as it looked before 1900.

She rented a room on Temperance Street for the following Tuesday, and asked that a fire be lit in the fireplace, and hot tea be ready to serve her clients. On Tuesday morning, she put on a red-haired wig bought from the hairdresser's, applied lots of powder and rouge to her face and was ready.

When she reached the house on Temperance Street, the front door was wide open and people were running outside, shouting, "Put it out! Put it out!" Smoke poured out of the windows on the upper floor, and a servant bounded up the stairs with a bucket of water.

"The grate wouldn't work," said the landlady when she saw Vic standing at the door. "Ruined the curtain. The chimney's no good."

Vic would not be able to have a fire in the fireplace, after all. The flickering firelight would have created such a cozy atmosphere. Oh well, she would have to make do.

As soon as the smoke cleared, she sat in her easy chair ready to greet her first

Credit: City of Toronto Archives, Fonds 1244, Item 698

Gypsies, or Roma, migrated from Europe to western Canada, then gradually moved east to make their living in large cities like Toronto.

client. She did not have long to wait. So many clients came by that morning that Vic was reminded of the saying, "There's a sucker born every minute!"

There were women, old, young and middle-aged; widows and widowers; businessmen, men of no business, and men who had no business being there. All wanted to be duped; all wanted to hear good news.

As Madame Vanier, Vic used her imagination, a pack of

cards, and a strong French accent. A businessman came to see her. With a worried expression, he told her that he was having a tough time making his business work, and she turned over her cards one by one, pretending to study them.

"Have no fear," she told him. "You will become very wealthy, Monsieur."

Many more asked about their love lives and she told them that they would soon find their true loves. To one hopeful woman, she said, "Do not worry, Mademoiselle. I see a handsome man in your future."

The morning went by quickly and then there came a brief lull. Vic gazed out the window for a few moments. Across the street, she saw a young man coming out of the Veterinary College and crossing the street toward her house.

"Are you Madame Vanier, the fortune teller?" he asked when he was invited into the room.

"Please be seated, Monsieur," she said, then shuffled her deck of cards, laid some cards out, and pretended to study them. "Monsieur, there is here a dark-haired woman who is supposed to be a very good friend but she is, in truth, an enemy."

 ic may have modelled "Madame Vanier" after a famous French fortune teller, Madame Marie le Normand, who was so accurate in her predictions that thousands of very powerful people came to see her. Fortune telling dates back to 4000 BC but today, it is not a term that people use very often. Instead, people call themselves psychics, tarot readers or clairvoyants, although some practitioners in Europe still use palm reading, tea leaves, and crystal balls. Today, people consult horoscopes to look for the same information that the 19th century fortune teller might offer.

The first fortune-telling machine was made in the 1890s. Customers would slide a dime into the slot, and out would pop a fortune, delivered by a mechanical figure behind the glass.

Vic looked at the young man out of the corner of her eye to see if he had any reaction. He was nodding his head with excitement so she must be on the right track.

"Monsieur, there is a property that you will one day inherit, but it is claimed by this woman."

Credit: Albert Anker

Fortune tellers used playing cards and tea leaves to read their clients' futures.

The man pounded the table with his fist. "I knew it! She's the worst enemy I've got. She's my own mother!" He leaned forward and gazed at her cards. "Go on, let's see what's going to become of it."

"Now, Monsieur," said Vic, inventing happily, "a fair young man will help you out of your difficulties. He's been a good friend to you."

"Yes, I know just who you're talking about. He's been a good friend to me," said the young man. "He's paid for my schooling and I'll reward him for his help," he vowed. He sprang out of his chair, gave Vic his coins and left whistling cheerfully, believing in a good future for himself.

A tall woman dressed in black entered, and asked Vic if she could find some property owned by her son who had died a short

Credit: City of Toronto Archives, Fonds 1244, Item 9014

"Read your palm, Miss?" A fortune teller offers her services at Jackson's Point in Toronto.

while ago. Vic was stumped. She gazed at the cards, wondering what to say. "I'm sorry Madame. I cannot find this property. Perhaps he already sold it," she said at last.

Husbands asked her if their wives really loved them. Wives coolly asked her how long their husbands would live and what date would they become widows.

A young woman told her she had a boyfriend who was shorter than she was. She had been out with him three or four times. Would he propose to her?

"Have no fears," Vic told her. "You have won his heart. He will soon propose."

Vic gave good news to everyone and thought perhaps it was time to deliver some bad news for a change. At this moment, an older woman entered and sat down in front of Vic. She wanted to know if she would ever meet someone who would love her. Vic's answer would haunt her for a long time after and make her feel a terrible guilt at what she told the woman. "No, I am sorry to tell you this. You will never marry," she answered as she studied her cards.

In the woman's eyes, she saw the hope turn to horror and despair and the woman quickly left. Vic wished with all her heart she had not said those words but it was too late. For the rest of the day, while she listened to the funny, peculiar, sad, bitter and even painful stories of her clients, she remembered that woman and hoped some bachelor would find her, somehow.

Vic spent the day listening to clients whose stories drove her almost to tears as well as laughter. She could have filled a book with the problems she heard that day, ranging from the ridiculous to the sorrowful. At the day's end, she realized that fortune tellers had "a great and terrible responsibility" in their chosen profession as the "nineteenth-century witch." All in all, the day had been a great success but she vowed that never again would she use words to hurt someone for the sake of her column.

A GIPSY ENCAMPMENT.

The term "Gypsy" has existed for centuries. Though it is commonly associated with the Romani people, it also carries broader stereotypical meanings, not all of them positive. Today, some consider it to be a less-than-acceptable term.

Vic played the fortune teller for only a day, but she knew there were hundreds more real fortune tellers, not only in Toronto, but across Canada. At the time when Vic was writing her column, the Romani people, known then as Gypsies, had begun to migrate to Canada from Eastern Europe and later, from Argentina. They were even given free land in the Canadian prairies on condition that they clear the land and farm, but they did not stay there long. They soon roamed to eastern Canada, working as horse traders, showmen, and peddlers.

Many Victorians thought that this wandering was a romantic way to live, but there was prejudice against them, as well. Gypsies were "foreigners" and did not seem to have any recognizable religious beliefs. The Church was very important in Victorian society of the 1890s, so people were both suspicious of them, yet fascinated by their lifestyles. It may have been that there were so many restrictions among men and women about the "proper" way to live, that the Gypsy way of life seemed very freeing.

The idea certainly appealed to Vic.

Do you know more about Vic from reading about this experience? What have you learned about her?

Chapter 3

Vic Steinberg, Bookseller

Vic groaned when she looked out of her window and saw heavy rain. Not the perfect day for selling books, but the letter of instructions from the publisher made it clear that she was to go out in any weather for the next six days, and to make sure she worked full days. She was to investigate the job of bookseller and sell at least three books that day. What was it like to knock on doors and try to sell a book? What kind of books did most people like to read? These were some of the questions she must answer in her column.

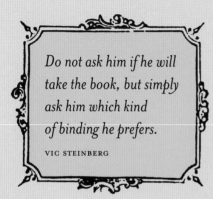

Do not ask him if he will take the book, but simply ask him which kind of binding he prefers.

VIC STEINBERG

Vic had always loved books and reading. As a child, she read so much that her aunt thought it was bad for her. "She'll come to no good with all that nonsense crammed in her head!" Vic had always wanted to be a writer, and even as a young girl she somehow knew that to write well, she must read as much as she could.

Vic thought about her aunt and smiled. If she could see Vic now, she would blame it all on too much reading.

Vic put on her jacket and went down to the newspaper office.

"Are you sure you want to give me this assignment, today?" she asked. "Look at this awful weather!"

"Are you giving up before you've started?" asked the editor. "There are some men here who could do the job if you can't."

Those were the only words Vic needed to hear. She would

Credit: McLeod & Simpson

The Queen's Hotel stood at the corner of Front and Yonge Streets. It was torn down in 1927 to make room for the Royal York Hotel, which still stands today.

soon show him! She was just as capable as any man. She vowed to sell a dozen books that day as she set out into the rain, making her way to the Queen's Hotel where Vic asked for the manager, Mr. McGaw.

"Mr. McGaw is in the billiard room," said a receptionist. "He wants to know if it's pressing."

"Yes, very pressing," said Vic. She was a member of the Press, after all.

While she waited, she rehearsed what she would say. "Mr. McGaw, I have here a book that I wish to show you." How would that sound? No. Not right. Maybe she would try the French accent she had used when she was "Madame Vanier."

"Monsieur would pardon Mademoiselle for taking him away from business," she whispered to herself, trying it out. That sounded better.

The receptionist returned to say that Mr. McGaw could not see her, but to please make an appointment for another time.

Vic turned and walked out into the rain once more.

The wind was beginning to rise, threatening to blow her umbrella inside out. She hurried along to her next stop—the home of Reverend W. F. Wilson. He lived in a grand manse on Bloor Street. Vic rang the bell and a maid ushered her into the front parlour. There she found Mr. Wilson sitting in a rocking chair and resting a bandaged foot on a stool.

He's very handsome, thought Vic as she shook hands with him and introduced herself. Mr. Wilson had fine dark eyes and a welcoming smile. He beamed at her, until she took out her book, then the smile left his face. She guessed he must be disappointed that she was not asking advice or seeking religion, but simply selling books.

"No, I haven't read this book, but I've read reviews about it," said Mr. Wilson, implying that he didn't like the reviews.

"But those are only little descriptions. This book is the full story about the life of the Prime Minister of Canada, his early life, his rise to fame—"

Mr. Wilson interrupted her. "The Conservatives buy this book. I don't think I want it."

"But it's wise to read about the life of any good man, don't you think, whether you are Liberal or Conservative?"

"Doubtless, but I can let you know some Conservative Party members who might like to read it," said Mr. Wilson.

Vic thanked him and left. She had better sell a book soon or the boys at the paper would have a good laugh. The rain was pelting down as she rushed along to a factory on King Street to talk to the owner, Mr. Piper.

Mr. Piper bustled up to Vic, looking very kind and interested in what she had to say. They shook hands and he pulled out a chair for her. Vic laid the book on his desk and said, "I'm sure you're a reading man, and this is a book you can't do without."

"I've already ordered that book," said Mr. Piper, then leaned over his desk and looked closely at Vic. "Haven't we met before?" he asked.

Vic's heart sank down to her boots and she had a sudden fit of coughing, holding her handkerchief close to her face. Would he remember her? For it was one of the gentlemen who had come to have his fortune read. He had asked if his business would succeed and make him a rich man.

"Yes, your face seems very familiar. What is your name, again?" he asked.

"My name?" stuttered Vic. "My name is...er...Rose."

"And you live in Toronto?"

"Yes, that is at present, I'm selling my books here."

Today, Front Street doesn't look at all the way it did in Vic's day.

Credit: MarcusObal

"But you're not a Canadian?"

"Don't I look Canadian?" asked Vic.

"You're American, I think," said Mr. Piper.

"Yes, I believe I am."

"Well, if you have any other book, I'll be pleased to look at it," offered Mr. Piper. "But I'm not especially interested in this one."

Vic quickly left his office. That had been a close one!

It must be the weather—everyone Vic spoke to gave many reasons for not ordering the book. "I have a copy." "I've already ordered it." "I'll order it next winter when I have time to read."

She saw Mayor Kennedy on Front Street, running up the steps of City Hall and called out to him, waving the book.

"I've already ordered it," he called, then disappeared through the door.

Vic went back to the newspaper to face the teasing. She had to admit it—as a book agent, she had not been a howling success.

Credit: Wikimedia Commons

Libraries and bookstores stocked their shelves with books from Britain and the United States. There was something for every taste, from the mysteries of Arthur Conan Doyle to the fantasies of Robert Louis Stevenson.

What did the editor say that galvanized Vic into action? What does this tell you about Vic's belief in herself as a woman living in a "man's" world?

Selling books was a tough job, as Vic's experience showed, but it provided an income to those who were willing to try. Booksellers in the Toronto of 1895 sourced their books mainly from Britain and the United States, but there were some up-and-coming Canadian authors that Victorian women loved to read. Catherine Parr Traill and Susanna Moodie were making a big impression with their books about surviving in the Canadian wilderness. Everyone wanted to read the American writer Stephen Crane's *The Red Badge of Courage* published in 1895. For different tastes, there were the science fiction books of H.G Wells—*The War of the Worlds* and *The Time Machine*. Rudyard Kipling's *The Jungle Book*, R.L. Stevenson's *The Strange Case of Dr. Jekyll and Mr. Hyde*, Arthur Conan Doyle's *Adventures of Sherlock Holmes*—all reached Canadian audiences during the 1890s. One of the top sellers at this time was Mrs. Isabella Beeton's *Book of Household Management*, an advice book that appealed to Victorian wives and homemakers, but it is unlikely that Vic Steinberg would have chosen to read it!

Chapter 4

Vic at the Tavern

Men stood at the long bar, deep in conversation. There were salesmen in shiny suits, lawyers and judges in fine wool suits; men from all walks of life sipped ale together and Vic, the only woman in the room, stood right alongside them. But no one so much as glanced her way. Her disguise was working. The bar she was leaning on ran the length of the room and in the long mirror behind it, she could see her image. In a man's clothes, she looked like a young college student with a clean-shaven face and innocent gaze. She was wearing a suit that just about fit her. She had belted and pinned the pants high up on her waist and put some stitches in the jacket sleeves so that they were not so long.

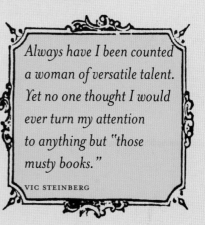

Always have I been counted a woman of versatile talent. Yet no one thought I would ever turn my attention to anything but "those musty books."

VIC STEINBERG

Vic was here because she had a column to write. She had often seen crowds of men pushing into the taverns along Yonge Street, but "respectable" women never entered them. Vic had always wondered what these places were like inside. What did men talk about when no women were present? It would be interesting to eavesdrop and observe the effects of drinking on family men.

The only way for her to enter a tavern without inviting attention was to dress as a man, slip inside, and observe the place for herself. It would be a good stunt for her column, so she persuaded Ned to help with her disguise again. At 9:00 that evening, she and Ned pushed through the door of a Yonge

Credit: Benjamin Vautier (1829–1898)

Working class men in shabby suits drank alongside bankers in expensive clothes.

Street tavern. They made their way through the crowded room and headed for a quiet corner, where Vic propped herself up at the bar and pretended to read the *Toronto News*. With her head bent over the paper, and a cap pushed down over her forehead, it was easy to look around the room without being noticed.

She noted the guard rail running along the top of the bar, probably to keep the tipsy drinkers from accidentally smashing their glasses to the floor as they lurched about, she thought. A trough ran along the front of the bar filled with sawdust. Occasionally men who chewed tobacco spat their quids into the trough, or threw down their cigar stubs and cigarette butts.

Across the room stood a table covered with a clean white linen cloth. In the center was a large bowl of chopped cabbage. Beside it was a plate piled high with slices of bread and cold roast beef. A pot of salt, a pot of mustard, and a pile of forks placed in a glass of water completed this "banquet." Customers stepped up to the table, took a piece of beef, placed it on a slice of bread, dropped some salt on it, rubbed the mustard spoon over it, then munched this snack along with forkfuls of cabbage. Vic noted that most customers forgot to give the fork a bath in the glass of water before again dipping into the cabbage. "They would throw all that to the dogs if they were at home," thought Vic. "If their wives put that in front of them, they would look at it with startled surprise. They act as if they have the stomach of a goat and the head of a donkey!"

She winked at Ned, and wandered over to the table. Her rule of thumb was to try everything once. But a closer view of the table and its offerings caused her heart and stomach to fail her. She couldn't eat this rubbish. "Flunked!" she told herself, and moved back to the bar. The barman asked, "What'll it be, sir?"

"A seltzer," she answered. The bartender stared in mock surprise and she thought, "Flunked, again!"

"I'm on the wagon," she explained. "Trying to turn over a new leaf for the New Year."

"You're still young and tender," replied the barman as he served up the sparkling water. "There's time, yet."

One of the many derivations for the phrase "on the wagon" is that politicians used bandwagons to make their speeches in public streets. People who jumped on the wagon were those who supported the politician's cause. It eventually came to mean that if someone was on the wagon, he or she was in support of a social cause; in this case, against drinking and for sobriety.

Vic shrugged, took the glass and moved back to her corner to gaze around. There were all classes of people in the tavern from smooth-faced youths to shrewd businessmen. Working-class men wearing shabby, dirty coats stood side by side with bankers and judges in expensive, glossy clothes. Silk ties and old slouch felt hats bobbed companionably at the bar. Streams of men poured in through the swinging doors, some gulping a drink and leaving quickly, others lingering to talk and joke with friends. Some called out, "Stay and have another!" to departing friends. Others seemed to be waiting for an invitation to drink. Many leaned stupidly against the bar trying to "get straightened up" before going home to their wives.

"I tell you what," said one of these. "I'm going to swear off. I said I'd do it years ago when I married her, but the stuff gets such a hold on a fellow. I swear off the stuff this very night."

Vic set down the glass of seltzer and folded up her newspaper. "I haven't done too badly as a man, so far," she said to Ned. "Time to move on."

She and Ned strolled down Yonge Street toward a more fashionable tavern on King. Vic thought how strange it felt to be wearing wool tweed trousers, vest and jacket, but how good to be freed from the damnable corset and be able to

Credit: Library and Archives Canada

move and breathe without that tight feeling. It was past ten o'clock, and Yonge Street was alive with crowds of men and the occasional scarlet woman. She felt nervous and was glad that she was in disguise and that Ned was with her. She strode along with confidence.

Two stylishly dressed men stood outside a hotel on King Street, carelessly twirling their

"Cappers" stood on Toronto street corners at night, enticing victims to play a game of cards in gambling saloons.

canes and puffing away on cigarettes.

"Come on in, sirs," they called out. "Have a good evening with us."

Under the streetlight, Vic could see their waxed mustaches, smoothed to a point at each end. In spite of their good clothes, she knew these were "cappers" looking for victims to enter a gambling saloon nearby. She was aware that these men worked with the dealer to rob the strangers at their card table. Sixty-five

Credit: Don Smith

"Give me a light, Jack," said Vic as she tried to smoke her first cigar.

policemen usually walked the Toronto streets at night, but that was hardly enough to catch the assorted thieves and criminals to be found doing their business.

Young men and girls, out for an evening stroll, occasionally jostled her as they stopped to push and wrestle with each other or exchange jokes, taking up the whole sidewalk. Vic was relieved to reach the swinging doors of the tavern at last.

"I dare you to try a scotch," murmured Ned to her as they walked in.

Ever ready to accept a dare, Vic stepped up to the bar. "A hot scotch," she requested of the bartender. He passed her the steaming drink and she looked at it, pausing for a moment. Ned noticed her hesitation and gave a mocking laugh. "I'll show him!" she thought. "Do or die." She raised the glass and took a gulp. The fumes from the scotch hit her square in the eyes and nose, and she spluttered and coughed. What to

Credit: Hemrich Bros. Beer

Hemrich Bros.
BEER

The Beer with *The*
Mellow Flavor

PURE—HEALTHFUL
INVIGORATING

**USED IN THE PALACES OF THE RICH
AND THE COTTAGES OF THE POOR**

*In spite of the Temperance Society, beer companies put out their
message that drinking was good for your health.*

do? She couldn't drink this. She stepped to the end of the bar and when no one was looking, poured the drink into a spittoon. Ned turned away, hardly able to keep a straight face.

She bought a cigar, squeezed it, sniffed it, bit off the cap and spat it into the trough nearby, copying her colleagues at *The News* when they smoked at work. Now it was time to smoke the thing. "Give me a light, Jack!" she called to the bartender and marvelled at her sudden burst of bravery. One puff, two—that's enough! She threw it down, coughing. "Can't you give a fellow a better weed than that?"

"Aw, come on, now," said the bartender. "There's no better cigars in Toronto than them."

Vic had no idea whether it was good or bad. She had never smoked one before. She gazed around the room. Unlike the first tavern, groups of wealthy businessmen in fine suits stood drinking wine, smoking cigars, laughing and joking. The talk was just the same as it was in the other tavern.

"What's yours?"

"I'll have a lager."

Credit: Wikimedia Commons

HERE LIETH
A
TEMPERANCE
MAN

A noted temperance
man lies here
The green turf o'er
his head
No man e'er saw
him on his beer
Till after he was dead

WATER

This cartoon gently pokes fun at the Temperance Movement.

"Here's with you, old man; here's hoping we'll drink many another social glass together."

She was sure the same conversations were taking place in bars all across the city. She had seen and heard enough. One look at the headline she wrote for the next edition shows exactly what Vic thought of taverns:

All sorts of men holding up the bars and making hideous fools of themselves. Amusing, pathetic, disgusting.

How does the bartender describe Vic's appearance and what does this tell you about her approximate age? You probably have a good idea of Vic's personality. What words would you use to describe her? By commenting on men's behaviour in taverns, what does Vic show about her personal attitudes to drinking?

Newspapers of this time not only helped to satisfy their readers' curiosity about the wider world—the newest discoveries, world-famous celebrities, and any topic about the changing world around them—they also sent a message to their readers as often as they could about the pitfalls of drinking. Vic's newspaper, *The News*, often preached against drinking, because in Toronto society, it was believed that drinking led only to broken families and lost jobs. The Temperance Movement was an organization that advised people to abstain, and Vic was a card-carrying member. With her daring and sense of humour, Vic was able to share her disgust with drinking yet still make her readers laugh.

Chapter 5

Vic, the Fencers, and the New Woman

"You think it looks easy?" said a woman fencer to Vic. She held her sword tightly in her gloved hand, and spoke through her face mask. "So did I, when I first began. You just try it and you'll soon see it's not so easy."

So Vic tried it.

"Place your right foot so," said Vic's instructor, "and your left foot so." Vic stood with her feet twenty inches apart and both knees bent, in a position that did not feel graceful.

With his guidance, she "deceived a parry" and "lunged in carte"—at least that's what her instructor told her she had done. At the end of her lesson, Vic understood that it was not as easy as it looked. She couldn't wait to tell her friends about fencing. She had learned all this in only her first lesson, and most wonderful of all, the costume must not be worn with corsets! Without the hated corset, she felt free to move in any direction and did not have to endure the uncomfortable feeling of being squeezed.

"But what is the use of fencing in these days?" asked Vic. "No one challenges anyone to fight a duel."

"It's a grand exercise," answered the instructor. "It can be played by young or old, weak or strong, man or woman and

> *Toronto should be proud of the growing desire for athletic life among women. I am a great believer in physical exercise and muscular development for women. Nature was kind to me and equipped me for the battle of life with a remarkable constitution.*
>
> VIC STEINBERG

gives the best results in the world. It can improve your health and make your muscles flexible, strong, and graceful."

She watched two other women who thrust and lunged with their swords. They wore bloomers, a short skirt, and a loose-fitting padded jacket with brass buttons. All the reports that Vic had heard about such sports being unsuitable for women were proving to be wrong. The women did not look "mannish" as critics of women fencers said. It was an exercise that helped women to be even more graceful and healthy at the same time. It was the "New Woman"—athletic and healthy, no longer weak but still feminine.

The invention of the three-wheeled cycle made it socially acceptable for women to ride bicycles.

"I certainly do feel the freedom of movement," said Vic, thinking about the corset she was forever complaining about. "But I did feel clumsy in some of the movements."

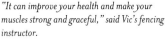

"It can improve your health and make your muscles strong and graceful," said Vic's fencing instructor.

"That's because you're not an expert," said her instructor. "If you ever watch an expert fencer, you will see how graceful the sport is."

In her column that day, Vic wrote about fencing, the New Woman—and corsets.

"Dumbbells develop the arms and chest, dancing develops the legs, but fencing develops every muscle of the body to work in perfect harmony," she enthused. "The spread of fencing will help to drive a nail in the coffin of that enemy of womankind: the corset which makes the body from the hips to the chest and up, inert and dull."

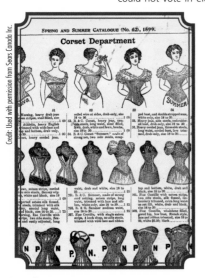

Is Your Figure Stylish?

You can see a difference between personal style and common fashion. Style is the air, the pose, the grace—the movement that is your own—through every change of fashion. Fashion is common to every woman who can pay for it. Only one corset helps the development of that individuality which is true style: La Grecque Corset. Not a hard mold for the figure. It helps the figure to mold itself.

DUQUESNE

Vic advised, "The corset should never be worn during exercise, for it has been shown that the wearing of even a moderately tight corset adds from fifteen to eighteen beats to the heart per minute during the exercise."

Vic was happy to throw away her corset whenever she could, and taking part in a sport such as fencing was a very good way to do it.

Vic called herself a "New Woman." She broke the rules about how women should behave and where they should go.

It was an exciting time for women. They were beginning to want a career besides wife and mother and were not afraid to try. Like Vic, women were forming strong opinions about what they were able to do. They could not vote in elections, but many of them were asking the question, "Why not?"

But something very basic prevented women from exploring new ways of living their lives: their clothing.

In the 1890s, Vic and other women had to follow the fashion rules and wear clothing that stopped them from moving freely. Married women were usually confined to the home as wives and mothers and their clothes served only a decorative purpose. Fashion designers believed that the corset helped women to look the best they could be, giving them a smaller waist and an hourglass figure. Vic often complained in her column about corsets, and with good

This ad promises ease and comfort to the wearer. Vic Steinberg did not agree. She was happy to toss aside her corset as often as she could.

reason. Long dresses with full skirts emphasized women's figures but women couldn't breathe properly if their undergarments were fastened too tightly. It was difficult even to sit down in comfort. Not only that, dress sleeves were sewn tightly across the arms to restrict full movement. All these annoyances prevented women from bending and moving in a natural way and from exercising.

But all this was beginning to change.

The New Women of Vic's time believed they were equal to men and they soon began to prove it by taking part in sports or working outside the home. They were eager to try their hand at the new technology: the telephone, the elevator, the cash register, the typewriter. They ventured out into the workplace to try their luck. It was a battle at first—men were hired before women more often than not, but women soon began to find employment as saleswomen, secretaries and telephone operators. All of these new adventures helped women to rethink their clothing. If the "New Woman" wanted to ride bicycles, fence or play hockey, they had to trade their long skirts for bloomers: baggy trousers worn under a shorter skirt.

Men and some more traditional women were quick to criticize this new trend. A letter to the editor of the *New York Times* in 1896 complained that the New Woman "...dresses like a man, as far as possible, thereby making herself hideous...the next step will be to wear

Women did play hockey as early as 1891, but they played in long skirts. The skirts offered a surprising advantage because the players would spread out their skirts as they stood in front of the goaltender—a manoeuvre that helped to catch the puck before it hit the goal. The wife of Canada's Governor General, Isabel Stanley, and her daughters, were fans of the game and they urged Lord Stanley to donate a cup to men's hockey. No one could ever have predicted that women would soon be wearing more practical clothing and joining women's hockey teams throughout Canada. Becoming skilled in this and other sports offered women more power over their lives.

Credit: City of Toronto Archives, Series 330, File 228, Sheet 5R

Women's clothing tended to prevent them from enjoying sports. These hockey players seem encumbered by their long skirts but there was an advantage—they could catch the puck in the folds.

Credit: Wikimedia Commons

Ride a STEARNS and be content

While some women wore traditional long skirts to ride bicycles, others were beginning to rethink their clothing. The "New Woman" cyclist preferred to trade her skirt for bloomers.

What new facts have you learned about Vic? Why does she think fitness is so important for women?

her hair short and adopt a mustache...to work by man's side and on his level and (still expect to) be treated with the chivalry due her."[2]

Being a "New Woman" herself, Vic and others like her championed women who cast aside restrictive clothing and opted for fitness, because with fitness came better health and the confidence to explore different kinds of lives.

It is no wonder that Vic's column was so popular. She gave women a glimpse of the freedom they could have if they dared to try.

Chapter 6

Vic Steinberg, Bachelor Girl

It was mid-morning when Vic collected her girlfriend, Gretchen, a nurse at one of the Toronto hospitals. The two planned to go shopping so they sent for a horse and sleigh, much as today we might phone for a taxi.

"Take us about town for an hour," said Vic to the driver, "then down to Murray's on King."

It was a grey February day in 1895, and the snow was piled high along the sides of the road while soft flakes still drifted down. As the hack trotted along, the two women passed the grand mansions and public buildings along Bloor Street, then turned south along University toward King Street. The sight-seeing ended at King, and the two entered some stores, buying small knickknacks, then dropped into a restaurant for lunch.

> To keep on my dignity for one whole afternoon, to indulge in an amount of small talk and say a number of pretty things which mean nothing, is not wholly agreeable to my nature.
>
> VIC STEINBERG

"Will you have some blue points?" asked Vic, meaning oysters.

"Yes, blue suits me very well," said Gretchen dreamily, thinking about a dress she planned to buy.

The rest of the day, the two spent visiting friends. They sat in front parlours, talked about the weather, their health, terrible servants, and politics, and joked about the cost of another friend's bonnet. They talked to younger friends who were thinking about getting married, and to older friends who never would get married. They kissed new babies and made everyone very happy

Credit: City of Toronto Archives, Series 1201, Subseries 5, File 2

Vic's friend Gretchen worked in a traditional profession for women. This is the uniform she probably wore as a nurse in 1895.

with their visits, although by this time, Vic was feeling miserable. It was hard work for her to make small talk about fashion or babies. As a working woman with a well-paying job, she had little patience for other women who preferred a dull domestic life that included housework and babies. She cheered up at six o'clock, when visiting hours were over and they could go to a German club for dinner.

"You never ate a wiener?" she asked her friend. "They're a German sausage; not poetry, but they're delicious. I have a friend over here, and I'm sure if we drop in and see him, I can coax him into taking us into the club. What do you say?"

The two went to the Liederkranz Club, a restaurant and bowling alley on Richmond Street, with their male friend where they had a couple of wieners and a glass of lager. In the evening, the three went to see the play "Robin Hood" at the Grand, and after dinner Vic and Gretchen sauntered home while Gretchen told her stories about her patients at the hospital.

It had been a late night and a typical one for Vic Steinberg. But now she was ready to write a new story for her column entitled "Bachelor Girl."

hornton Blackburn escaped to Toronto from slavery in the 1830s and lived in "The Ward" with his wife Lucie, waiting on tables at Osgood Hall. There, he heard some lawyers talking about a fantastic new form of transportation they had discovered in Montreal. It was the taxi cab. The idea captured Thornton's imagination, and he set up a taxi cab company of his own that within a few years made him very wealthy. He did not forget his old neighbourhood, and was able to buy up several blocks of land within St. John's Ward, creating low-cost housing for other African Canadians who migrated to Toronto from the United States.

To be called a "spinster" meant that a woman could not find a husband to take care of her. People looked upon spinsters

Credit: www.istock.com

Oh, how times have changed since Vic's days!

with pity, but the term "Bachelor Girl" was fast coming into use for the unmarried or not-yet-married woman and Vic was quick to use it for herself. Vic called herself a "Bachelor Girl," another name for the "New Woman,"—someone who had chosen to turn her back on becoming a wife and mother for the time being. Bachelor girls lived in large cities like Toronto, shared an apartment or a boarding house with other working girls, and worked as sales clerks in department stores, as telephone operators, or as secretaries.

Vic was one of many women who were taking steps to change the way they lived their lives. They were not looking for the support of a husband. They knew how to take care of themselves, and were happy to be independent, to throw away the corset, and to wear more practical and useful clothes. This "Bachelor Girl" trend caused many angry arguments about the "proper" role of women at that time, but people like Vic led by example, and other women soon followed.

Vic goes out "on the town" buying whatever takes her fancy, dining at a restaurant for lunch, and going to the theatre in the evening. Victorian women who entered clubs alone were considered to be "loose," so Vic seeks a male friend to accompany them. In this column, Vic gives the reader some information about her life. What have you learned about her?

Chapter 7

Vic at the Tie Factory

Vic held the slippery needle as sweat trickled down her neck. She wiped her face with the back of her hand and tried to concentrate on the tiny stitches. Her back ached from sitting in one position for two hours. The girls around her, bent to the same task without complaints, were sewing quickly with their nimble fingers. Their pile of finished work was growing ever larger, compared to Vic's two finished ties. She must try to catch up. She had stepped into one of the most difficult jobs she had ever taken on for the sake of her column and it had all come about because of a letter from one of her readers.

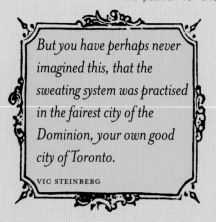

But you have perhaps never imagined this, that the sweating system was practised in the fairest city of the Dominion, your own good city of Toronto.

VIC STEINBERG

Dear Editor,

As Miss Steinberg travels so much around the city, it would be worth her while to go and visit some of the shops and factories where poor girls have to try and make a living.

There is one factory on a downtown street where they advertise quite often. When a girl goes there, she is given to understand that she will make from four to five dollars per week. When she is hired and set to work, she is told she will have to pay fifty-five cents for thread, five cents for soap, and pay for all the needles she may break.

Every two weeks, for the making of a dozen of ladies' underclothes, she will get twenty-five cents. With such poor wages fancy what a girl will have when her two weeks are up when the above items are deducted from her pay! There is also another shop where girls are told that they will make as much as nine or ten dollars a week.

I tried it as well as the others. I worked for two weeks, and all I got was twenty-five cents. I did a lot of work but was never paid for it. It didn't matter how well it was done, they would find fault with it and then we would be told we could go so as to make room for more new girls.

By doing this all the time, they get their work done for almost nothing! By giving this space in your paper, you will confer a great blessing on poor working girls.

The letter writer was giving a true picture of the Toronto sweatshop.

Vic read her reader's letter with interest. She had heard of sweatshops but she had never believed they were this bad. Did bosses really treat the girls so unfairly and send them away with little or no pay for hours of work?

Well, it was time to find out!

She had scanned the newspaper for notices calling for seamstresses and chosen one with an address on Spadina Avenue that stated, "No Experience Required." She put on her worn grey

Credit: Johnston, Frances Benjamin, 1864-1952

Women were paid piecemeal (by the piece). They had to fill their quota by the end of each week in order to receive their wages.

dress, the one that had always disguised her well as a poor working girl, and took the streetcar to Spadina Avenue, then walked a few blocks south. The red brick building had dingy, dirty windows, and broken steps. Vic walked into the showroom where a glass counter displayed silk and cotton ties of every colour and style. A man stood at the back counter, bent over some papers. As soon as Vic entered, he glanced at her, then pointed up the stairs.

"Go up to the cutting room," he called. Vic climbed the creaking steps. At the top, there was a room with long tables, and men cutting away with their scissors at rolls of fabric. Two men stood nearby in conversation.

"There's a lady here," called one of the cutters to these gentlemen, "come to speak to you."

One of the men in conversation gave Vic a dismissive glance. "I'll tend to you directly," he said. He turned his back to her, as if he didn't have time to waste on a mere working girl. Vic waited for ten minutes, then the man sauntered over, hands in his pockets.

"Well?" he said.

"Could you find some work for me?" asked Vic.

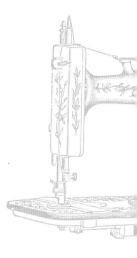

"Name?"

"Victoria Smith."

"Can you sew?" he asked.

"I can always try. I'm willing to learn," answered Vic.

After a few more questions, he took her up a narrow, creaking staircase to the third floor where about twenty girls sat at long tables. "This is where you'll be working," he said. "You can start on Monday."

Vic looked at the tired, pale faces of the girls who were bent over their sewing. No one looked up at her, and a forewoman walked up and down the rows, picking up pieces of silk and examining them, then tossing them back down. The windows were encrusted with grime and the light was poor. It was very hot as none of the windows were open.

Vic had always disliked sewing and needlework. She imagined the forewoman would fling much of her work down in disgust.

In the 1890s, the ten leading occupations for women were servant, dressmaker, seamstress, tailoress, saleswoman, teacher, farmer, housekeeper, laundress, or milliner.

The following Monday morning, Victoria Smith arrived at the tie factory, and climbed the two flights of stairs to the hot room under the eaves. The forewoman placed her at a long table between two girls whose heads were bent over their work.

"Where are your needle and scissors?" she asked.

"I didn't know I was to bring any," answered Vic.

"I'll give you some, but you'll need to pay for them out of your first wages. Can you do a slip stitch?"

"If you would show me, I'm sure I can learn."

The woman snorted with impatience. "Here," she said, reaching into her apron for a spool of thread, a needle and some scissors. She quickly threaded the needle and picked up a scrap of fabric, then stitched so quickly that Vic could hardly see what she did.

"Practise on this," said the forewoman and left the scrap for Vic.

Vic looked closely at the stitches the woman had made. The girls beside her all had a box of silk pieces that were to be sewn into ties. Vic jumped when the forewoman came back and plunked a similar box in front of her.

"Start on these," she said.

Vic's job was to hem the ties, then sew a lining on the back. She watched the girl beside her, then tried it herself. The needle was like a slippery piece of steel that jabbed and poked the tips of her thumb and fingers as she drew it through the fabric. The first hour seemed as long as a day. She squinted at her stitches in the dim light, felt the sweat trickle into her eyes, and her back ache from her bent position. She felt miserable, bored, and frustrated till she wanted to scream. By the end of the day, she had made only four ties. How much will they pay me for this? she wondered. She asked the forewoman.

"You're only paid by the dozen," said the forewoman, looking at Vic's four ties. "The rate is 5 cents for twelve ties."

Vic did a swift calculation. For today's work, she had earned 1 and 2/3 cents!

Vic looked around at the girls seated at the tables. They wore the plainest dresses and it was obvious

Credit: Asai Chu

Victorian women considered decorative sewing to be a womanly skill.

Credit: City of Toronto Archives Fonds 1244, Item 1364

Victorian women valued office jobs. Such work offered security and steady wages.

they did not have any of the pretty frills and trinkets that girls loved.

"How long have you worked here?" she asked the fair-haired girl beside her.

"Just two weeks," she answered. "We see new faces every day. Many of the girls only last a day and never come back."

"Do they pay the girls fairly for the work they do?"

The girl lowered her voice. "Sometimes. Many have to do their work over and over before they get anything for it." She stared at Vic's work and shook her head. "You may have trouble getting anything for that," she said, and turned back to her sewing.

Vic looked at the crooked stitches she had made. The girl was probably right.

Vic went back to the tie factory every day for a week. She was getting faster, her stitches were better, but by the end of the week she was making only about eighteen ties each day. On Friday, it came time to ask about her pay. The forewoman took on a hard expression as she looked at Vic's work for that week. "You've twenty-four more ties to sew. You will have to finish them all before you ask for your pay."

"So will I be paid next week?"

"We send in our checks for our work on Friday, and get our pay Monday. Since you have not finished this pile, you won't be paid until a week Monday. Don't forget they will hold back money to pay for soap and for the needle and scissors I gave you."

When Vic left the building that day, it was for the last time. They would not be seeing her face there again. At least, she had that choice to make, but these poor women and girls did not. What sort of life must they have?

———— ✺✺✺ ————

Sweatshops were small workrooms crammed with workers who sewed fabric into clothing. In the 1890s, factory owners contracted their work out so they didn't have to pay for the electricity or heat. It was cheaper to use workers to do the work of machines.

By 1900, less than ten percent of the labour force in Canada belonged to a union. The Ontario Factory Act in 1884 directed a 60-hour work week for children over the age of 14, but employers usually ignored this directive.

Factory owners sent their fabric, sometimes already cut and ready to be sewn, to other bosses who ran the sweatshops and hired girls and women as seamstresses. These women included thousands of immigrants from Europe who were newly arrived in Canada and trying to make ends meet.

The bosses gave women the lowest and most boring paid handwork to do. Since mothers at home taught their daughters how to sew, this was seen as just a "domestic skill," like doing laundry or washing dishes, and was not given much value outside the home.

The seamstresses worked for 50 to 60 hours per week, up to 10 hours every day. If you were to enter a sweatshop of that time, you would see mothers and their young daughters working

Credit: Jozef Israels

Many believed that to be a good wife and mother, it was important for women to stay at home

side by side over their stitching, because children often worked alongside their mothers to bring in a little more cash to support the family.

Men were always paid more than women to do the same kind of unskilled work and many eventually became bosses themselves. Women never could become bosses and there were no unions to protect women workers. The factory owners did not feel responsible for the daily lives of workers in the sweatshops. They pretended not to know about the awful working conditions or the low pay.

In Vic's time, women were not expected to work for pay outside of the home unless they had to. Instead, their roles were to do "good works" such as helping the sick or homeless, and being a good wife and mother. People thought that women had different, gentler natures than men, and different kinds of work suited their natures. An editor of an Ontario newspaper in 1889 told his readers, "Nature has made them dissimilar…Man, the rough and rude; woman, the gentle, modest and kind."[3]

The News' sister paper, the *Toronto Mail*, often quoted from the Bible to show that women held an important place in the home. People believed that by staying out of the workplace, a woman could be a devoted wife and mother, and have a good influence on her family. Working women had no protection from terrible conditions or from bosses who paid unfairly. These problems did not discourage women from finding jobs outside the home. Usually they did not have any choice. No matter the attitudes of the time, many women needed the work to survive.

By the turn of the century, workers formed unions that helped women to get fair treatment, a shorter work day, and more pay. Women like Vic forged ahead toward a new definition of themselves, and their place in life.

At the time Vic was writing her column, there were many women who were beginning to push for equal rights with men. One of these was Clara Brett Martin. She was the first woman to practise law in Canada. The regulations at that time barred women from becoming members of the Law Society of Upper Canada, because they were not considered to be "persons." In 1897, after lobbying for changes to overturn the regulation, Clara won this right for women. With such an advancement, it was much easier for women to push for better working conditions and ultimately to form unions.

Look back at the previous columns about taverns and rugby games. Is Vic beginning to change her perspective, from the merely frivolous to much more serious topics? She is no longer just entertaining her readers but seems to have a deeper purpose. What social issues is Vic exposing in her columns?

Chapter 8

Vic Steinberg at the County Jail

Vic entered through the side door of the Don Jail, and Governor Green greeted her. He led Vic to the glass-ceilinged rotunda. There, he pointed to a square of black flagstones where prisoners used to be flogged. The punishment of flogging was no longer given at the Don Jail, but prisoners were sent to the Central Prison, "where they have a first-class flogger," said Mr. Green.

"May I have one peep at Clara Ford?" asked Vic.

"You can have a look for a second, but do not speak to her," warned the Deputy.

He introduced her to the matron of the women's prison.

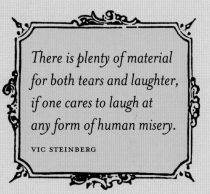

There is plenty of material for both tears and laughter, if one cares to laugh at any form of human misery.

VIC STEINBERG

As soon as the Governor had left them, the matron turned to Vic. "I thought you were a "case," when I first saw you," she told Vic. "Your eyes are so large and bright. We often have ladies who have suddenly become insane brought to us to wait for an opening in the asylum. I thought you were one of them."

Vic laughed at this. "I think my head is all right," she told the matron as they walked toward the women's quarters. Vic found that the women's cells were neat and clean with lots of fresh air circulating.

In the receiving room, the matron chatted about their newest prisoner, the notorious Clara Ford, recently accused of murder.

Toronto had been plunged into a panic when one of its

Credit: City of Toronto Archives, Finds 1244, Item 1152

The Don Jail still stands today. In Canadian jails in the 1890s, there was a rule of silence. No one could speak without permission and the punishment for talking out of turn was flogging. This practice was later abolished.

citizens, Frank Westwood, a young man from a wealthy family, was killed by a gunshot wound. The police force could find no clues that could lead them to the murderer. The chief of police asked Sir Arthur Conan Doyle, author of the Sherlock Holmes mystery novels, for help. Doyle replied that he couldn't help them because he was used to writing a solution first, then creating clues that would lead to this solution. He was unable to work in reverse.

Their suspicions had eventually fallen on Clara Ford, a woman who, strangely enough, had something in common with Vic Steinberg: She often disguised herself as a man. Clara was an African Canadian who used to go about the city dressed in men's clothing and toting a gun. The police could not understand what her motive for murder was but they put her in a cell in the Don Jail.

"When I came into the room one day, Clara Ford was sitting on that sofa," said the matron. "She said to me, 'Well, this is the first time I was ever in a police station.' The girl looked respectable," continued the matron, "and I asked her what she was arrested for. 'Oh,' she replied. 'They say I killed young Westwood, but I didn't.' She also told me her picture would be in the papers. 'It will be in *The News*, anyway; they always have lots of pictures.'"

The matron remembered how nervous she had been to meet a suspected murderer. "I was too nervous to eat much of anything, but Clara was quite cool and ate a hearty dinner."

She selected a key from a large ring and unlocked the door to Clara's cell. The cell seemed like a cozy little room with its five small beds and a floor carpeted with rugs.

"Such an interesting face," thought Vic as she looked at Clara. The woman she was gazing at showed no interest in Vic. She was sitting on a bench at the end of the room talking with two female guards. Vic would never have guessed that this prisoner

Credit: Wikimedia Commons

The chief of police asked the famous writer of Sherlock Holmes mysteries, Sir Arthur Conan Doyle, for help in solving the Clara Ford mystery.

was accused of murder. She did not look upset, just very calm and cool. Around her lay books about adventure and travel which the matron said she loved to read.

"She's a model prisoner," whispered the matron, "very quiet and patient. Who would ever guess...?"

The Don Jail was believed to be haunted by a blonde-haired ghost. Her name was Lilly Kelly, and she hung herself in one of the tiny cells for women in the west wing. Guards on the night shift reported seeing her spirit floating through the air in the main rotunda.

"If the accusations are true," thought Vic, "that hand lying carelessly in her lap is stained with the blood of a fellow human being."

Vic saw many women that night, one in jail for stealing an overcoat, another for being drunk and disorderly, but the glimpse she'd had of Clara Ford stayed with her and she followed the case with interest.

In her next column, Vic gave a good report of all she had seen and how impressed she was by the women's section of the jail. She noted that the prisoners were neat and clean, very well cared for.

"I've studied the Toronto [police] system. I've examined every shaft and cogwheel in the whole machine. I've spent hours at Police Headquarters and in the jails. I've seen the prisoners come in. I've seen them marched off to the cells...and the sights I witnessed were well worth seeing."

"The prisoners are comfortable and contented," she wrote. "The Toronto jail is not an exceedingly unpleasant place in which to spend a month."

───────── ༺༻ ─────────

The Toronto Don Jail of Vic's time was a dark, imposing building, a place where criminals and drunkards alike spent time.

Built in 1858, it is still standing today on Gerrard Street near the Don River, with many modern additions. A second prison, the Central Prison for men, located in the west end between the railway tracks and west of Strachan Avenue, was completed in 1864. This building offered a humane way of holding prisoners because it was well ventilated and let in natural light, although some cells measured only one by three

Credit: Wikimedia Commons

Some jail cells measured only one metre by three metres in area.

metres in area. Rules were strict.

Prisoners were not allowed to talk without permission and were flogged if they broke the rules. They spent twenty-three hours in their cells, and one hour in the exercise room. Conditions in prisons gradually improved over the years and flogging was eventually discontinued.

What became of Clara Ford? Several months later, at a sensational trial, and to everyone's astonishment, a jury found Clara Ford not guilty, and she was freed. She left Toronto and was never heard from or seen again. The mystery surrounding Frank Westwood's murder was never solved.

CLUE

Vic hints that she has spent hours at Police Headquarters and in the jails; many more than the few hours she wrote about in her column. What does this tell us about Vic's background? Is it probable that before she became a columnist, she was just one of many reporters "on the beat," chasing paddy wagons, or the Black Maria from courtroom to jail or sitting in the courtroom taking notes? This was the daily life of hundreds of newspaper reporters who were always looking for a good story. Vic must have been an exceptionally good reporter to have earned a promotion to newspaper columnist.

Chapter 9

Vic Steinberg, Servant Girl

Vic had heard her married friends complain about their servants. They stole; they were lazy and rude. What about the servant's side of the story? Was it true that servants in the grand homes were exploited? So often, she had heard women say, "I cannot get a good girl!" or "Why are there no trustworthy, reliable maids?"

Vic imagined the servant's life must be very hard; they did so much work for so little pay. Why would women choose such a career?

Everyone Vic knew seemed to have complaints about servants, but had anyone ever asked the housemaids for their opinions? Vic had never heard their complaints. What was it like to work for society women, she wondered. Was it just as impossible for servants to find a trustworthy, reliable boss? There was only one way to find out.

> *The servant of today is considered a slave— forced to humor every whim of the woman over her, bound down by the hundred and one little set laws of "madam," called upon at every hour of the day or night to do her bidding; and in nine cases out of ten asked to do work which belongs rightfully to man and not woman.*
>
> *The servant was made by the same God as was her mistress; that her soul was made just as white, her heart with as womanly instincts, her body with as many weaknesses as that of the woman she serves.*
>
> VIC STEINBERG

"A young woman, trustworthy, reliable, thoroughly domesticated, desires a situation as housemaid, parlor maid, or general; references exchanged."

Vic looked over her ad, satisfied that it was short and to the point. She took it to the copy editor's desk that very morning for placement in the evening's classified column.

There were no answers to her ad the next day, but on the second day, Vic found seven letters waiting for her in the newsroom. Vic made two piles. Mrs. Rogers of Prince Arthur Avenue wanted an upstairs girl to take care of three children and help with the sewing. Vic placed this letter in the "yes" pile. Mr. Williams of King Street, a widower, was boarding at a hotel but was tired of being without a home and wanted a housekeeper to help take care of little five-year-old Timmy. This one she placed in the "no" pile. Two other letters asked for character references from her former employer. Vic placed these with Mr.

The architectural style of this Victorian house was typical of its time. Such houses are still standing in present-day Toronto.

Williams' letter. She had no references to give. The next letter was written by an elderly woman who wanted a companion. Another woman wanted a nurse and housemaid. These two were "no." If she was to gather enough information on the lives of domestic servants, it would be best to take a job that only involved housework duties.

Vic opened the last envelope, written in fine handwriting. Mrs. Bates on College Street promised a good home and every comfort in exchange for a girl who was reliable and capable. She did not ask for references, so Vic placed this one on the top of the "yes" pile.

Vic Steinberg thought carefully about her next disguise. She hurried home and dressed in her plainest dress and found some

Credit: Joseph W.Molto

Credit: Toronto Reference Library

In the front parlour, there was no end of things for Vic to lift and dust and polish.

old scuffed boots for her feet. She wrapped her wool tweed cape around her, pushed her bangs under a woolen tam, and then boarded the College streetcar.

It was a cold February morning and there were a few late commuters on their way to work, bound for the offices along King Street. A few minutes later, she rang the bell at Mrs. Bates' door. She stepped back to gaze at the house that might be her place of employment for the next few days. It was a large red-brick building fronted by white pillars, and guarded by two stone lions gazing out toward the street. A rounded bay window gave the home a graceful appearance.

She had been in such houses as a guest but never gave a thought to the servants who cleaned them. This was such a large house to keep clean, thought Vic as she waited.

The door opened and a young girl peered out. She had a mop of untidy yellow hair and a smudge of white flour on her cheek. "You the girl come to hire?" asked the girl, her glance taking in Vic's plain dress and scuffed boots. Without waiting for an answer, she beckoned her inside and closed the heavy oak door behind her. "Wait here," she called as she hurried off. Vic stood in a grand hallway lit by wall sconces. A half-opened door to her right revealed a formal parlour with plush couches and polished mahogany. A very big house to clean! She hoped there were more servants than the slim young girl who had opened the door.

The lady who came down the stairs looked her over with a sharp-eyed gaze. She was tall and dark-haired and wore a haughty expression, as though she had better things to do than talk to servant girls. "Come with me," she said, leading the way down the hall and into a back parlour. "Sit down." She pointed to a plain wooden chair near the fireplace and Vic sat down and waited. The woman took a seat in the plush armchair opposite.

"Your name?"

"Victoria, ma'am. Victoria Smith."

"Have you worked as a housemaid before?"

"No, ma'am." Vic gazed at the floor, trying to look meek and lowly. "But I am domesticated and will give you no trouble."

"Where are you from?"

Vic was ready with her story. "My family has a farm in the country. I'm used to hard work."

"Well," said the woman, "I will try you for a week and if we are suited, you may stay. I will take you upstairs and show you your work."

She led the way along the hallway and up the stairs. "You will use the servants' stairs on every other occasion," she said as they went up the grand staircase. On the second floor were four large bedrooms, a bathroom, and a long hallway. "Servants' rooms are up there." She gestured to a little stairway at the end of the hall. "There is a maid in charge of the first floor. Your work will be to keep all the rooms on this floor tidy, make the beds, sweep, dust and arrange, help to dress and take care of the two younger children, answer the door, wait on table, and help me with the weekly mending."

"What wages will you give?" asked Vic.

Credit: www.istock.com

"I would like you to wear black dresses in the afternoon," said Mrs. Bates to Vic.

"Five dollars a month at first, and I will raise it to six if you are suitable."

Not very much, thought Vic. But she was to be given a room and meals.

"What religion are you?" asked the woman sharply.

"Does it make any difference?" asked Vic.

"I won't have you if you are a Catholic," snapped the woman. [4]

Vic felt anger rising, and forgot for a moment that she was a servant. "I don't belong to any church. It's not important to me."

"Not belong to any church?" repeated Mrs. Bates, her eyes flashing with astonishment and horror. "Well, the sooner you join one, the better! You will come to my church on Sunday."

Vic had to bite her tongue. "Yes, ma'am," she replied. "May I start tomorrow morning?"

"See that you are here by eight o'clock," said Mrs. Bates. She pushed a bell beside the fireplace and the girl who had answered the door came into the parlour. "Fanny, this is the new housemaid. You will give her instruction beginning tomorrow. You may show her out," she ordered.

Vic was hurried down the hall to the servants entrance. At the door, she spoke to the girl. "I'm Victoria. I'll see you tomorrow."

"You may not see me," said the girl. "I plan to collect my wages tomorrow and whether I stay is another matter."

"You don't care for it, here?" asked Vic, but the girl gave her a gentle push and shut the door firmly behind her.

Vic woke up very early the next morning, put on the same grey dress and scuffed boots, and boarded the College streetcar. She was soon knocking on the door at the servants' entrance to Mrs. Bates' house. Fanny, the kitchen girl opened the door to her.

"You'd best go up right away and dress the children for school," she urged. "Leave your bag in the kitchen."

"You're still here, after all," said Vic.

"Just for now," said Fanny. "Off you go. The mistress is waiting."

Vic's morning soon went by in a blur. After making sure the sleepy and complaining children were dressed, fed, and sent off to school, she swept and dusted all the rooms on the second floor. There was so much to lift and dust and polish; little china figurines, delicate bowls, brass lamps—there was no end to it. By ten o'clock that morning, Vic felt as though she had done a full day's work. But it wasn't over, yet. She went downstairs to the kitchen to ask Fanny what to do next.

"You had better hustle," chided Fanny. "You haven't started on the first floor, yet."

"The first floor?" said Vic. "But I was told to be in charge only of the second floor."

"Then you were told wrong," said Fanny, up to her elbows in dishwater as she stood at the sink, washing breakfast dishes. "It's a

Domestic help in grand houses were expected to cook, sew, clean, iron, and take care of the children. They were only given one half day off every week.

good thing Mrs. Bates has gone out for the day or she would be right angry that it is taking you so long."

Vic hurried to the first floor where she dusted the front and back parlours and the sitting room, set the table for the children's lunch, polished the silverware, and completed several other tasks before 1:00. The long day seemed never-ending, but Vic had little time to rest. She was given a lunch of stale bread and a slice of cold beef before she was set to more tasks. By 8:00, Vic longed for bed, but Mrs. Bates told her she must wait up until her sister and brother-in-law came home. Vic sat in the

Credit: Charles Keene

Servants did not usually keep their jobs for long. The work was hard and the hours were long.

cold, drafty hallway from 8:00 until 10:00 that night, waiting to answer the door to these members of the household, then sank gratefully to sleep on a hard little cot in the attic. The next morning the whole routine began again.

"You're doing very well for someone with no experience, Victoria," said Mrs. Bates the next day, "but I would like you to wear black dresses in the afternoon, not grey."

Those were the only words of praise Vic heard from Mrs. Bates. At the end of that week, Vic gave her notice, saying she must return to her family since her mother was ill. Mrs. Bates was not pleased.

"Do not expect a reference from me," she snapped and thrust some coins into Vic's hand. "This is all you get for so little time in my household."

Vic took the proffered coins, tempted to fling them in the

woman's face.

She was writing her column in her head as she turned and left Mrs. Bates' house for the last time. Now she understood so much more about the demands of domestic service. Mrs. Bates had treated her like a slave, making her do work that was hard and physically demanding, expecting her to do her bidding at all hours of the day or night, and insisting that she always address her as "Madam," as though Vic was a lesser person with no rights of her own.

Mrs. Bates had demanded that Vic be of the same religion. Was this right? Was it kind to insist that Vic have no visitors? What about friends? If a girl was to have a friend, why must she meet that friend on street corners? Why was domestic work considered to be the lowest kind of work when it was really such an important part of making a home? Why did employers treat their help as though they were lowly beings worth nothing?

Now she understood why Fanny, and domestic servants like her, did not keep their jobs for very long. It was because of the long hours, the hard work, and the low wages.

———— ⚬⚬⚬ ————

As a servant girl, Vic was offered the wage of $5.00 per month. This amount included her room and meals. What is that in today's dollars? The sum of $5.00 would give the spending power today of $129.27 per month. Although a servant earned so little, she would not have the expenses of a more independent working woman. Servants would need to pay for

Vic's earnings from reporting gave her much more spending power. She probably started out by earning $1.00 every time she wrote an article. If she was on a full-time salary, she would earn $20.00 every month, a very good income for a woman of those times.

Here's how Vic, newspaper columnist, might spend some of her earnings in 1895.

A women's tea gown	$1.00
A silk blouse and long wool skirt	$4.50
Rent (per month)	$5.00
Groceries : 6 rolls bread	0.05¢
1 lb. fish	0.08¢
15 potatoes	0.10¢
3 lb. oatmeal	0.10¢
6 eggs	0.13¢
1/2 lb. tea	0.18¢
2 lbs. chops or a steak	0.20¢

Credit: Toronto Public Library

How to Wash
with
The "1900" Washer

THE "1900" WASHER CO.
437 Yonge Street,
TORONTO, CANADA.

The invention of the washing machine in 1900 made housework less strenuous for servants and housewives.

Vic says she always hears complaints about the servant problem. She has visited grand houses as a guest. It is likely that she knows middle- to upper-class women who are wealthy enough to hire servants and to complain to Vic about them. Does Vic herself belong to a more privileged class of people? If she were poor or lower class, she probably would not know such women. Vic often takes the College streetcar and she boarded it to go to Mrs. Bates' house. College Street was the area of middle- to upper-class residences in Toronto in the 1890s. Did Vic live on or near College Street?

their clothing and might send what was left of their money home to support their family. Cooks like the one who worked for Mrs. Bates earned slightly more than other servants, and they were valued more highly for their special skill.

As Vic thought about her column, she considered how she had been made to work from early morning till late at night with only one or two afternoons free. The attic room where she slept had been so cold and drafty and she was sure that it would be hot and airless in summer. Vic had learned about the strict curfew that she and other servants in the house had to observe. If they were not home by 10:00, they were locked out of the house and usually dismissed.

In her conversations with Fanny, she heard stories that the lady of the house often set traps for servants to test their honesty, like leaving something valuable lying around to see if they would steal it. If anything went missing, the servant would be fired whether or not she were responsible. It is no wonder, thought Vic, that domestic servants only took work in a household if they had no other way of earning a living. Many found that working in a shop or office gave them more freedom and it was easier work. Men were already finding better jobs outside domestic service in factories and offices.

Vic penned all these thoughts in her next column. The headline read, *Vic Steinberg as a Servant Girl: The Reason Why Most Girls Prefer "Shop" Work to "Service" in Private Residences.*

As Vic wrote her column, she was determined to expose the unfairness she had witnessed and to inform those people who complained about their domestic servants that there were two sides to every story. If they did not know this already, they were about to find out.

Chapter 10

Vic Steinberg, Shop Girl

"Have you any vacancies in this store?" Vic asked the manager.

She stood in the hiring office of a large department store on Yonge Street, and she was wearing a smart but plain day dress. She knew that if she was going to report on the working conditions of shop girls, she needed to look presentable to get the job.

The manager, a young man with a kind manner, looked her over from head to toe. "Name?" he asked.

"Victoria Smith."

"Which department?" he asked.

"I would take any position," replied Vic. "Clerk, bookkeeper, cashier, but I think I would prefer being a clerk."

Vic did not care where they placed her. She only planned to use her eyes and ears and write about her experiences.

> *The life of a shop girl, with its early and late hours, its monotony, its rush and hurry, its constant strain on mind and body, is not by any means an easy one.*
>
> — VIC STEINBERG

"Fill out this form and I'll see if it's satisfactory," said the manager.

There were many questions on the form. "What age are you? What weight? What height? Do you board, or live at home? Are you married or single? What is your father's occupation? How is your health?"

The manager looked over Vic's answers, and seemed to find her suitable.

"We'll start you off in fabrics, Miss Smith, and see how you do there."

Credit: Wikimedia Commons

A shop shows counters piled with a wide variety of fabrics. Victorian women were accustomed to selecting material and sewing dresses for themselves.

Vic joined two other young women behind the bargain counter and they showed her how to cut the bolts of fabric, and how to measure the cloth. Vic hoped this work would be much easier than her work as a domestic servant. Fanny, the cook at Mrs. Bates' house, had told her that she was going to hand in her notice and apply for a job in a department store. This had given Vic an idea for her next column—was the life of a shop girl as easy as it looked?

As the morning went on, Vic dealt with customers who were fashionably dressed and very demanding. She began to dread dealing with women customers because they were so choosy, they argued, and they took forever to decide on a colour. They tended to be rude, speaking to Vic and the other shop girls with a haughty manner and never saying "please" or "thank you." Vic soon learned why the shop girls preferred helping male customers. Men would never argue with their advice about the fabrics and colours that Vic privately knew were not the latest fashion.

The other girls advised her to smile pleasantly at the men and tell them, "It's quite the newest thing out."

It was true. Male customers believed everything she told them, and, along with the other girls, Vic invented stories and urged them to buy fabric for their wives even though the colours were not in style anymore. "What colour hair does your wife have? Fair? Then I'm sure this colour will suit her very nicely," Vic would say, pointing to hard-to-sell cloth in a vibrant purple. But her plans backfired, because an hour later, these same men would bring back the fabric and whisper, "If you wouldn't mind changing it. She didn't seem to care for it."

It is likely that Vic Steinberg applied for work at either the T. Eaton Company Limited (Eaton's), or the Robert Simpson Company Limited (Simpson's). Both were thriving department stores on Yonge Street and the stores were rival companies for many years.

During five-minute breaks, Vic talked to the girls she worked with and heard their stories. Some came from poverty and were struggling to make ends meet. Many had left their jobs as domestic servants, hoping for better working conditions. One girl, Elizabeth, supported her alcoholic father and brother, and lived in St. John's Ward, the slum district in downtown Toronto.

"What on earth are you doing here?" came a voice on the other side of the counter. It was Vic's best friend, Gretchen.

"Hush! Don't say a word," she whispered. "If you want to

buy that silk, I'll handle it, but don't give me away!"

Her friend giggled and pretended not to know her.

Vic found herself in the same situation many times that day.

"You? Working here?" came a voice from the other side of the counter, and Vic would explain that no one must know she was from a newspaper.

Conditions in the big Toronto department stores became much better for working women from the late 1890s and onward. Eaton's and Simpson's offered health services, boarding houses, and even financial help to women during times of illness. Helping women in this way led to the belief that these stores sold only the best quality products because their staff was well cared for.

Vic soon became used to dealing with customers, handling money, writing bills, and measuring fabric, but when the gong sounded at the closing hour, and as the six hundred female employees rushed to get their coats from the cloakroom, she heard the same sigh from everyone, "So tired!"

No wonder there was a question on the application form asking, "Are you in good health?" It took strength and stamina to stand at a counter for ten hours. Shop girls had the legal right to a stool to sit on when they felt tired, but Vic saw no stools behind the counter. No wonder the girls were so tired and pale.

In her column the next day, Vic called these girls, "the footstools of society." She wrote that they were kinder and more honourable than the wealthy classes of women. Shop girls found themselves forced to find work no matter how hard, because they were trying to escape poverty, but they were determined to make their lives and the lives of their families a little better.

Vic also knew that women who did not have to work outside the home, living comfortably and supported by husbands, often thought of shop girls as "common" or low class. In her column, Vic wrote of her sympathy for the shop girls and all working girls because they were underpaid and unfairly treated. "The young women employed are refined, womanly, and agreeable," she wrote about the workers she had met that day. She stated that the more privileged customers on the other side of the counter were ill-bred, and bad-mannered to look down on working girls and criticize them so harshly.

Let me say right here that the majority of these girls are better (according to their advantages) more refined in mind, healthier in morals than many of the ill-bred, discourteous women of the better (?) classes whom they serve.

Vic hoped that her column would encourage the wealthy women to be kinder to their working "sisters," but maybe she had gone too far in her criticisms of upper-class women. This was the last column she ever wrote for the *Toronto News*. It was published on April 22, 1895, and though her readers searched the paper for her next column, they were never again to see her name in print.

While serving behind the counter, Vic met customers she knew. She had friends who were probably middle- or upper-class women with the leisure time to shop and it is likely that Vic came from the same background.

Why was this Vic Steinberg's last column? Did she marry? Was she fired because of her criticisms of middle- and upper-class women, the very readers who followed her adventures? Whatever the reason, her column disappeared and her byline was never seen again.

Epilogue

Glimpses of Vic

Vic Steinberg dropped many clues and hints about who she was. How many did you find? Do you have a clearer picture of her? Let's figure out what we know.

Vic lived on or near College Street, Toronto, shown here in 1894. Note the electric streetcar in the background.

Credit: Toronto Public Library

Vic lived on or near College Street, a middle- to upper-middle class area of Toronto. She probably started working as a court reporter before she was promoted to columnist with her own byline, and perhaps her more privileged background helped with this promotion. She was a single woman probably in her mid- to late-twenties. At this age, she was already a "spinster" in some people's opinion, but she considered herself to be a New Woman, someone who wanted and enjoyed the freedom to explore the changing world around her without being restricted to traditional women's roles. Her day off with Gretchen shows her carefree nature and fun-loving spirit. She enjoyed a challenge, and liked to step outside of things that she found confining, whether that be the corset, or the narrow world that women lived in at that time. She had friends among the upper-middle class, people with servants and spending power, and probably grew up among the same class of people. She disagreed with drinking and taverns and called herself a Temperance woman. She was a good writer who could reach out to all kinds of readers, men and women alike, and she wrote with humour. She was feisty and daring, not afraid to put herself into new situations. She had a youthful appearance—a

Credit: Wikimedia Commons

A cigar box ad pokes sly fun at the "New Woman." Women's clubs were usually very genteel and not at all like the scene depicted here.

barman thought she was a young student. She had a great sympathy for those less fortunate than herself and was interested in telling their stories and acting as their champion.

Vic Steinberg's columns contain other little hints about her life, her childhood, and her views on how women and men lived in Victorian Toronto. She often expressed her mischievous opinions about marriage and the recipe for success. "What kind of man makes the best husband?" she asked in one column.

Well, the first thing is that he have a capacity for loving—more than ten days!

Here is the sort of man who, in my opinion, does his share toward making an ideal marriage—one not less than six years older than yourself, not of necessity highly intellectual, but he must not be stupid. He must be temperate in all things but not a teetotaler. A man who likes his after dinner smoke and don't mind holding the baby on his knee.

He should not be too much wrapped up in his profession, for business success is clearly gained at the expense of happiness.

Last, and most important, he must be very much in love with you. Sprinkle this combination of good qualities with pardonable faults just enough to give a piquant flavour, you know, and then my dear, take him for better or worse with the chances greatly in favor of the latter.

Credit: Toronto Public Library

This Victorian neighbourhood can be seen today in the Cabbagetown area of Toronto.

It is obvious that Vic was a sensible woman with no delusions about love and happiness!

Vic shows a sense of mischief sprinkled with good common sense when she talks about marriage. She enjoys a little joke about husbands when she makes this comment about married life, so subtle that it almost goes by unnoticed:

*In one corner, perusing the **Evening News** sat a dark, handsome, stylishly dressed woman in company with a middle-aged man who was evidently her husband but who nevertheless, seemed to take a lively interest in her.*

No matter her topic, Vic found the humour in any situation. This sense of fun was always present in her writing. Here, she shares a letter that she says is written by J. Jug. The letter, of course, is her own invention.

Dear Mr. Vic Steinberg
I saw you at Hurst's hotel in St. Louis during a Press convention. You had on one of those high stove-pipe

hats and your hair was long. You had a corn on your middle toe and a round hole cut in your boot so it wouldn't hurt. You wore a navy blue suit with two large brass buttons on the back of the coat, but none on the front; your pants were considerably bagged at your knees; you wore spectacles; one of your eyes was a little sore and both very red.

Sincerely,

J. Jug, Altenburg, Missouri

Readers probably enjoyed this invented letter that poked sly fun at her own appearance as well as her readers' wild guesses about her.

While Vic would never have given away anything about her identity on purpose, she does reveal enough clues that tell a little about her. Take her description of herself during an evening at the opera. Two gentlemen seated in the row in front of her were looking through their opera glasses at a woman in the balcony across the theatre.

"Do you see that woman dressed in blue?" she heard one saying.

"Well, what about her?"

"That's Vic Steinberg, the *News* lady reporter."

Here, Vic gives away some details about her age, appearance, and place in society.

The woman who sat behind these two youths glanced at herself, gowned plainly in tweed, and then at the subject of conversation – a fair, slender maiden dressed handsomely in silk, who wore a pug nose and eye glasses. She had her head bent forward, this marvel of youth and beauty – and her chin was

Credit: Mary Cassatt

"She'll come to no good with all that nonsense crammed into her head," said Vic's aunt.

raised so that the woman looking toward her was able to get a good view of the face – and in it she saw no resemblance to her own.

Alas, Vic Steinberg does not gown herself in silk, nor is she the maiden of tender years. Thus, my young friend, am I spared the fate of being blue-stockinged.*

*A term given to the wealthy upper-class woman or a writer.

Readers might wonder about Vic's childhood and the reasons she eventually chose a writing career. We know that reading was one of Vic's favourite things to do when she was little. In fact, one of her aunts worried that she read *too* much.

One maiden aunt actually persuaded my parents that, "She'll come to no good with all that nonsense crammed in her head," and a dear old uncle…invariably voted me, "A peculiar girl, a very peculiar girl."

Vic sometimes hints that as a child, she was full of mischief— not surprising then, that she loved to wear disguises when she became a columnist. She wrote that she grew up in the countryside in a house complete with stable and servants; a member of a large family with many sisters. Maids and stable boys were part of her childhood experiences. Her sense of mischief seemed to come into play even as a young girl.

Lots of times I have thought I must be naturally, very wicked.

As a child, I never took kindly to obedience, my usual response to the command, "You must be good," being, "Don't want to be good – no fun in it."

The servants always knew who the culprit was whenever they found a broken window or even a lame horse.

If the windows were broken, it was "Vic" who had been pitching snowballs. If my father's best mare was one day found to be lame or dispirited, old Bowser of the stables swore, "It was 'er as done it, sir; she stole 'im out, she did." If the maid noticed with anxious eye that the pillow-slips were in need of darning it was "The little miss, ma'am, as 'ave been 'avin' a sham fight."

So Vic was a lively child and not an easy one to take care of, but she won the hearts of all those in her household.

Barnes, the chore boy, always took my part against those who voted me the black sheep of a large family, of good, bad, and indifferent girls, gaining thereby, a warm spot in the heart of the frisky, fun-loving maid then in her early teens.

It seems that not only did Vic grow up in a large family with servants, she was also much loved and fun-loving, and her childhood experiences led her to become the free-spirited woman we know as Vic Steinberg.

Many people thought they had identified Vic Steinberg, newspaper columnist, but they were usually wrong. Vic enjoyed overhearing readers wonder and make assumptions about her. She always pointed out with glee how mistaken they were, but she never tried to set anyone straight. It was her remarkable skill, to take on a disguise, to step into someone else's shoes, all the while observing and recording the lives that she witnessed, and the unfairness she found along the way. Vic was often deeply touched by people's misery and way of life, as she went about her work as a reporter.

I have seen with my own eyes all that is visible to the world of the sin, degradation, poverty, misery and squalor of the poorer and alas, vice-stained districts of a big city.

Credit: City of Toronto Archives, Fonds 1244, Item 8031

The slum of St. John's Ward was situated where the Eaton Centre stands today. Home to recent immigrants, it was overcrowded and its people lived in poverty, but hoped to work toward a better life.

Her column disappeared in 1895 and she never again used the pen name Vic Steinberg. What happened to her? Did she resign? Was she fired? Perhaps she married and began to raise a family. Vic Steinberg's columns had been read and enjoyed by women and men alike, readers who appreciated her wit, her sense of mischief, and her ability to enter places that others might never go. One of her readers expressed this in a letter to Vic.

"I admire immensely (your column's) bright breeziness, so different from the milk-and-water, cut-and-dried conversational style so much in vogue in the women's department in Toronto. In your bright fearless, humorous style, you sandwich in the serious and the interesting, putting ideas in people's minds without arousing antagonism."

This was Vic Steinberg's gift; to be bright, fearless and humourous while striding into the thick of things and reporting on the sometimes terrible conditions she saw around her.

"I was well made up and acted my part to the best of my ability," said Vic. Certainly her readers could expect no less.

Credit: Toronto Public Library.

Vic ventured out into the Toronto streets to find stories that her readers would enjoy.

Vic Steinberg walked into places where women did not dare to go—saloons, smoking cars, sweatshops, prisons and slums, and she was never afraid to take risks. In fact, she enjoyed playing a joke as well as shedding some light on the awful working conditions that some women faced. She fooled many people and throughout it all, she shared her private joke with her loyal readers. She might be smiling yet if she knew that, to this very day in the 21st century she is still being noticed, and yet no one knows who she really was. That is just the way she always wanted it. And, after all, maybe it is not so important to crack all the secrets about this extraordinary woman.

When all is said and done, isn't it simply more interesting just to wonder?

Glossary

Asylum: The Toronto Asylum for the mentally ill was built in 1850 on Queen Street.

Byline: A line of text usually placed under a headline that states the reporter's name.

Cappers: Slang for card sharks intent on cheating their customers.

Collar band: Men's shirt collars were starched and separate from the shirt. Since there were few washing machines in that era, it was easier to exchange a dirty collar for a clean one.

Corset: An undergarment that shaped a woman's figure, made with laces and whale-bone stays.

Hack: An open carriage pulled by one or two horses.

Leg o' mutton sleeves: A style worn in Vic's time, the fabric of the sleeve is puffed out from shoulder to elbow.

Parlour: A room where the family gathered to relax. The formal front parlour was used to receive guests. The back parlour was informal and used by the family.

Sweatshop: A workroom where workers sewed piece-work clothing.

Temperance: A movement to reduce the use of alcohol in nineteenth and early twentieth century Canada. The Temperance Society was an organization that advised people not to drink, or if they did, to drink very little.

Index

Bibliography

Armstrong, Frederick Henry, *A City in the Making: progress, people and perils in Victorian Toronto.* Toronto: Dundurn Press, 1988.

Beetham, Margaret and Boardman, Kay, Ed. *Victorian Women's Magazine: An Anthology.* Manchester United Press, 2001.

Baskerville, P. Sager, E. The *Urban Unemployed and Their Families in Late Victorian Canada.* Toronto: University of Toronto Press, 1998.

Carter-Edwards, Dennis. *Toronto in the 1890s: a decade of challenge and response 1975.* (Canadian theses on microfiche; no. 22045.)

Chambers, Lori. *Married Women and Property Law in Victorian Ontario.* Toronto: Osgood Society for Canadian Legal History, 1997.

Darroch, Gordon. *Property and Inequality in Victorian Ontario: structural patterns and cultural communities in the 1871 census 1994.* Toronto: University of Toronto Press, 1994.

Development of Toronto's newspapers, Toronto: Toronto Board of Education, 1962.

Goad, Charles E. *The Mapping of Victorian Toronto: the 1884 & 1890 atlases of Toronto in comparative rendition.* Ontario: Sutton West, 1984.

Goheen, Peter G. *Victorian Toronto 1850 – 1900 Pattern and Process of Growth.* Chicago: University of Chicago, 1970.

Half-Century Anniversary Volume of the Mail and Empire, Toronto, 1872 – 1922. Toronto: The Mail and Empire, 1922.

Nicolson, Murray W. *The Other Toronto: Irish Catholics in a Protestant City,* 1850-1900, London Free Press, 1 March 1889. *Polyphony,* summer 1984.

Rutherford, Paul. *Victorian Authority Daily Press in Late 19th century Canada.* Toronto: University of Toronto Press, 1982.

Vic Steinburg columns: media room Robarts Library, Toronto. microfiche 1881-1919.

Souvenir of Toronto. Toronto: Valentine Pub. (19—) published for F.W. Woolworth Company.

Toronto by Gaslight: The Night Hawks of a Great City, as seen by reporters of "The Toronto News" (3rd ed.) Toronto: Edmond E. Sheppard, 1885.

Notes

---

[1] New York Times, April 8, 1896. *The New Woman Criticized; Is she unsexing herself and losing man's respect?*

[2] Beetham, Margaret and Boardman, Kay, Ed. Victorian Women's Magazine: An Anthology. *Young Women and Journalism, "The Woman Journalist"* (1864-1920). Manchester U. Press, 2001.

[3] Brown, George, *The Globe*. February 11, 1858

[4] Stead, W.T. Victorian Women's Magazine: An Anthology, Beetham, M. and Boardman, K. Ed. *Young Women and Journalism, "The Young Woman,"* vol. 1.1892. Manchester U. Press, 2001.

All other quotes and references are derived from the columns of "Vic Steinberg," *Toronto News*, at the John Robarts Library, Media Commons, microfilm (1881-1919).